50 THINGS YOU SHOULD KNOW ABOUT MUSIC

by Rob Baker

QEB

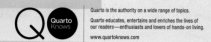

Design and Editorial: Tall Tree Ltd
Consultant: Malcolm Hayes

Copyright © QEB Publishing, Inc. 2016

Published in the United States by
QEB Publishing, Inc.
6 Orchard Road
Lake Forest, CA 92630

A CIP record for this book is available from the Library of Congress.

ISBN 978 1 68297 022 5

Printed in China

Words in **bold** are explained in the glossary on page 78.

CONTENTS

INTRODUCTION

From classical to pop, blues to rap, country to samba, music comes in an almost countless number of forms, and is enjoyed by people across the world. Over the centuries, music has become more complex, exciting, and varied. Yet, for all their many differences, all musical styles have certain elements in common.

MUSIC THROUGH HISTORY

Music has changed and evolved throughout history. Over time, new instruments have been invented along with ways of creating permanent records of compositions—first in written form and later as sound recordings. Music continues to change constantly as new styles, **genres**, and technologies emerge.

▼ A 2,000-year-old mosaic showing street musicians in the ancient Roman city of Pompeii.

WHY MAKE MUSIC?

Music is made for many different reasons. In ancient and medieval times, it was most often used for worship in religious ceremonies. It still has this use today, but also exists to provide entertainment, as an art form, and to sell products in advertising. Music is also featured in films and TV programs to help convey emotions and to accompany the action that is taking place on screen.

TYPES OF INSTRUMENT

All instruments have one thing in common: they make a sound which adds to the quality of the music. But the way they make this sound can vary. Some instruments are blown into, some are hit, while others have strings which are strummed, plucked, or played with a bow.

▲ Bongo drums are played by being hit by the musician's hands.

MUSIC ACROSS THE WORLD

Every country and culture has its own style and way of making music. It might have a fast **rhythm** or be slow and gentle. It may also include certain dances, costumes, or other rituals as part of the musical experience.

▼ The crowd watches a performance by the rock band the Who, at Glastonbury, UK, in 2015. Glastonbury is one of the world's largest music festivals.

How music works

WRITTEN MUSIC

Most parts of the world use the same system for writing music based on a five-line **stave**. The written music provides the musician with all the information they need to play a piece, including the **melody**, **beat**, **tempo**, and how loud or quiet parts should be. This means that a musician in Australia can write a composition and send it to a musician in Greenland who would be able to read and play it immediately.

The music now known as classical or orchestral music developed out of traditions begun in the middle ages. Over time, general rules have evolved about the numbers and sorts of instrument that should be used and how the music should be written and performed.

THE ORCHESTRA

In a classical **orchestra**, the instruments are organized into four groups: strings, brass, woodwind, and percussion. The instruments in each group are played in a similar way and often make similar sounds. For example, the brass section is made up of curved metal instruments, each with a small round mouthpiece. These four sections of the orchestra have their own characteristic style and work together to create a balanced and effective sound.

The orchestra
An orchestra has four sections: brass, woodwind, strings, and percussion (see pages 8–9).

Brass
Brass instruments are played using either valves or slides (see pages 10–11).

Woodwind and strings
Woodwind instruments are blown while stringed ones are plucked, strummed, or bowed (see pages 12–13).

Percussion
Percussion instruments are hit, shaken, brushed, or scraped (see pages 14–15).

MUSICAL SCIENCE

In scientific terms, all music works in the same way. When someone sings, an instrument is played, or a stereo plays a record, it creates a sound wave—a movement of air particles—that travels through the air to our ears. The frequency of the sound wave—how quickly it vibrates—determines whether we hear the sound as a high or a low **pitch**. High-frequency waves are detected as high-pitch notes, while low-frequency waves are detected as low-pitched notes.

◄ Plucking an electric guitar string causes it to vibrate, creating a sound wave which is then amplified electronically.

▼ An orchestra may have as many as 36 stringed instruments: 20 violins (divided in two between first violins, which play the melodies, and second violins, which play slightly lower notes), 10 cellos, and 6 doubles basses.

Written music
Music is written on a set of five horizontal lines known as a stave (see page 16–17).

Chords
Individual notes can be combined to form chords (see page 18).

Conductors
The conductor stands at the front of the orchestra directing the performance (see page 19).

Choirs
Choirs use differently pitched voices to create harmonies (see pages 20–21).

Orchestral instruments

The modern symphony orchestra combines many different instruments that are grouped into four main families, from the fanfare-like brass to the flowing strings. The conductor stands facing the orchestra and beats time to keep the musicians in sync with one another (see page 19).

(see page 19).

STRINGS

The string section is made up of violins, violas, cellos, and double basses. The stringed instruments are normally played using a bow, but they are sometimes plucked too. The bow is a wooden rod roughly 30 inches long, with 150 horse hairs strung between its two ends. The higher stringed instruments are usually used to play quick melodies, while the lower ones create deep, sustained notes and bass lines.

BRASS

The brass instruments consist of trumpets, trombones, French horns, and tubas. They are made of metal tubing that curves around so it can fit into a small space, making it easy to hold and play. Brass instruments help to make music loud and dramatic. They can also provide contrasting softer tones, as they can be played so they rise and fall in volume very quickly.

◀ *The trumpet is one of the most popular brass instruments.*

A large symphony orchestra can contain more than 100 musicians.

PERCUSSION

Percussion instruments are not used in every piece of orchestral music. The ones most commonly featured are the kettle drums (left), cymbals, shakers, bells, and the snare drum. Percussion makes the music sound more exciting and dramatic, and is usually heard during louder sections of a piece.

▲ *Kettle drums are usually played with felt-tipped mallets.*

▼ *The conductor stands in front of an orchestra, leading it through a piece of music.*

WOODWIND

All woodwind instruments are long and thin. They include the flute, clarinet, oboe, and bassoon. Originally, they were made of wood. Nowadays, flutes are usually metal and some clarinets are made of plastic. The woodwinds provide extra detail to the music, and the higher-pitched instruments can play the tune instead of the strings. Because they are played by covering holes with fingers that have been trained to move fast, woodwind instruments can be played very quickly.

▶ *The flute is played by blowing air over an opening.*

5

Brass instruments

Brass is a metal made from a mixture of copper and zinc, which can be easily shaped and curved to form the parts of an instrument. The larger open end of a brass instrument is called the bell. Its flared shape helps to **amplify** the sound. At the other end is a round mouthpiece, which the player puts to their mouth.

The first metal trumpets were made in ancient Egypt in around 1500 BCE.

VIBRATING LIPS

To play a brass instrument, a player has to vibrate their lips against the mouthpiece. As the air passes through the tubing of the instrument, it resonates, creating the sound. The player can tighten their lips to play higher-pitched notes, although they won't be able to reach all of the available notes using this method. So most brass instruments also have three valves, which can be used to change notes.

◀ *A musician plays the trumpet by vibrating her lips on the mouthpiece.*

WORKING VALVES

When pressed, a valve moves down to open up an extra section of tubing. This makes the total length of the instrument longer, which lowers the pitch of the sound. Each valve opens a slightly different length of tubing. Used in combinations, they allow the instrument to play every note in a **scale**.

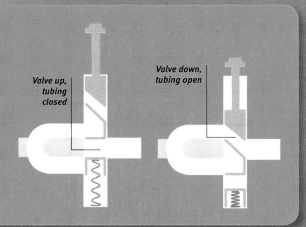

Valve up, tubing closed

Valve down, tubing open

TROMBONE

Instead of valves, the trombone has a long slide. When the player pushes the slide away from them, it extends the tubing, lowering the pitch of the sound. There are seven separate positions for the slide, which can be used to create different notes. The trombone is the only brass instrument that can play a *glissando*— sliding up or down from one note to another.

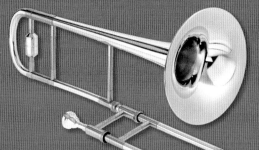

◀ *The trombone's slide makes it one of the longest brass instruments.*

UNUSUAL BRASS

There are several types of brass instrument that aren't normally featured in an orchestra. These include the flugelhorn, which is like a trumpet but larger, and the cornet, which plays exactly the same notes as a trumpet, but is shorter with a slightly different shape. Because it is compact and easy to carry, the cornet is commonly used in marching bands (see also the sousaphone on page 74).

▶ *A jazz musician with a flugelhorn, which plays the same notes as a trumpet, but has a bigger, fatter sound.*

4

Woodwind

The sound of many woodwind instruments is made by a musician blowing into a mouthpiece fitted with a device called a reed. A reed is a small thin strip of woody material cut from a type of stiff grass that grows beside rivers and ponds.

VIBRATING REED

When blown, the reed vibrates to make a sound. To change the pitch, the player covers holes in the instrument with their fingers—the more holes covered, the lower the pitch. Players needed long fingers to reach all the holes of early woodwind instruments. But modern instruments have pads that cover holes which cannot be easily reached.

▶ The woodwind section of a student orchestra, featuring bassoons (below), clarinets (bottom right), and flutes (right).

SINGLE OR DOUBLE

The clarinet has a single reed, whereas the oboe and bassoon use a double reed, where two reeds vibrate against each another. The flute is the odd one out. It doesn't have any reeds. Instead, the player blows across a small hole near one end, in the same way as you can blow over the top of a bottle to make a sound.

▲ The reed on a clarinet mouthpiece is held in place by a metal clamp called a ligature.

▲ An oboe's double reed is very thin.

Stringed instruments

There are many types of stringed instrument, but only a few of these are featured in the orchestra (see pages 8–9). All produce sound when their strings are vibrated, which is then amplified either acoustically by the instrument's body or electrically by another device.

HARP

The harp dates back over 3,000 years, and can be found around the world in all different shapes and sizes.

The concert harp has 47 strings, which are played with both hands. It also has seven pedals, which can be pressed to change pitches. To help the player find the notes, all of the strings which play a C are red, while the F strings are dark blue.

MINI GUITARS

Non-orchestral stringed instruments include the ukulele, a Hawaiian version of a traditional Portuguese instrument. It resembles a guitar, but is much smaller with only four strings instead of six. The word "ukulele" means "jumping flea" in Hawaiian, and refers to the fast strumming motion of the player. The banjo, which originated in Africa, has four to six strings and a round body with a skin stretched over the front, giving it a distinct sound. The mandolin is similar to both, but has eight strings, which are grouped together in pairs.

▲ The ukulele is much smaller and easier to hold than a guitar.

◄ A member of the country band, the Steep Canyon Rangers, playing a five-string banjo.

◄ A large 47-string concert harp, such as this one, has to be played sitting down.

Stringed instruments are played either by being bowed, plucked, or strummed.

Playing percussion

Percussion instruments are played by being hit, shaken, brushed, or scraped. They include all drums, cymbals, bells, and shakers. There are also tuned forms of percussion, such as mallet instruments and kettle drums, which can play notes that are at different pitches.

Ride cymbals

Crash cymbals

Toms

Hi-hat

Snare drum

Bass drum

▶ A drummer uses wooden sticks, or sometimes brushes, to beat out a rhythm on their instrument.

PLAYING THE DRUMS

A drum kit is a set of several different drums and cymbals played by a single drummer. A standard kit will usually include a snare drum, which has thin metal strips on its underside that vibrate to give a loud, crisp sound. There will also be a bass drum, which is played with a foot pedal and produces a low, booming tone, and a hi-hat consisting of two cymbals pressed together, which are hit with drumsticks or clapped together using a pedal.

The world's largest drum kit, owned by a drummer in the USA, is made up of 813 pieces.

MALLET INSTRUMENTS

Mallet instruments are so named because they are played using long sticks called mallets (or beaters). Hard mallets are used for a clear, bright sound, and soft ones for quieter tones. The xylophone is a mallet instrument made up of a series of wooden bars, which get smaller in size as the pitch rises. These are laid out like the notes on a piano, so a pianist can learn the xylophone quite easily.

▲ Striking the glockenspiel's metal keys with a mallet produces a bright, ringing tone.

OTHER MALLETS

The glockenspiel is played in a similar way to the xylophone, but is much smaller with metal bars instead of wooden ones. The marimba also resembles the xylophone, but usually has more bars (up to 60), and can play lower pitches. Although the modern marimba originated in Mexico, its ancestor is, in fact, the balafon from West Africa (see page 59).

▲ The long metal tubes below the xylophone amplify its sound.

KETTLE DRUMS

The kettle drums, also known as timpani, are different from most drums because they can be tuned to play particular notes. A foot pedal attached to the base is used to tune it by tightening or loosening the drum's skin. The timpani's low-pitched tones are often featured in orchestral works, providing rolling bass notes in louder sections of the music. A typical orchestra normally has between two and five timpani, all played by one musician.

▶ A pair of beaters sitting on a kettle drum.

How music is written down

Music is written as notes on a set of five lines known as a stave. A symbol called a clef at the start of the music tells the musician what pitches the lines and spaces represent. There are two main types of clef: a treble clef for high notes and a bass clef for low ones.

SHARPS, FLATS, AND NATURALS

♯ This is a sharp sign—it instructs the musician to play the written note a half step higher than normal.

♭ This is a flat sign—it instructs the musician to play the note a half step lower than normal.

♮ This is a natural sign—it shows that a note should be played as normal, neither sharp nor flat.

▼ Written music allows a musician to play a piece they've never heard before.

Notes that fall outside the range of a stave are written on extra lines called ledger lines.

16

MUSIC SCORE

A music **score** is filled with symbols telling a musician how a piece should be played:

KEY SIGNATURE

The **key signature** informs the musician what **key** the music is in by telling them how many sharps or flats they need to play (the black keys on a piano).

TIME SIGNATURE

The top number tells the musician how many beats to count per **bar**, while the bottom number tells them how long each beat should be. A 3/4 **time signature** consists of 3 **quarter note** beats per bar.

BAR LINE

This divides the music into bars—sections of equal length—and makes it clearer to read.

ACCIDENTALS

These are extra sharps, flats, or naturals added to the music where needed. An accidental only lasts for one bar, then the note returns to its normal pitch.

REST

This is where no music is played.

PHRASE LINES

These lines mark the phrases of the music— a group of notes which flow together.

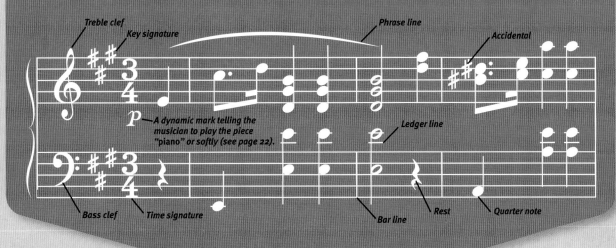

Treble clef · Key signature · Phrase line · Accidental

P — A dynamic mark telling the musician to play the piece "piano" or softly (see page 22).

Ledger line

Bass clef · Time signature · Bar line · Rest · Quarter note

TABS

Guitar tablature (or "tabs" for short) is another simple way to write music. Six lines are used to represent the six guitar strings, from highest at the top to lowest at the bottom. The numbers show the guitarist where to put their fingers. A "2" on the fourth line from the top (the D string) means that the guitarist should place their finger on the second **fret** to play an E. A "0" means that they should play an open string. Guitar tabs don't always show the length of each note, so the player may need to hear the music to know which notes are long and which ones are short.

▶ Tabs for four bars of guitar music.

8 ▶ Chords

A chord is made up of three or more notes played at the same time to create a harmony. Most Western forms of music, including classical, jazz, and blues, are based on melody lines played over chords.

MANY NOTES

Chords can be played only on instruments that are able to play several notes at once, such as the guitar or the piano. The most commonly used chords are major chords (which sound "happy") and minor chords (which sound "sad"). To play guitar chords, the fingers of one hand press down the strings in certain positions, as in the example below. The numbers tell the guitarist which finger to use.

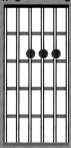

▶ A guitar chord diagram for an A chord. A "o" means the guitarist should play an open string, while an "x" means not playing the string at all.

A

◀ The neck of the guitar is marked out by metal strips called frets which show the guitarist where to put their fingers for each note.

▼ A pianist can use both hands to form chords, while a guitar player uses just one.

PIANO CHORDS

A pianist can play chords with the left hand, right hand, or both. In classical music, the chords are written down in full in the sheet music. In jazz and pop, however, the score may just provide chord symbols which the pianist can use to play along with the music. This is known as "comping" (short for accompanying). When comping, it is common for a pianist to play a three- or four-note chord with the right hand, then two bass notes with the left hand, an **octave** apart.

What does a conductor do?

The conductor stands in front of the orchestra where all the musicians can see them. Their main role is to set—and beat out—the time of the music. This ensures that the musicians start and stop together and keep in time with each other.

▲ The Italian composer Verdi (1813–1901) conducting his opera Aida in 1880.

9

The conductor follows a large musical score, which shows every instrument's part.

▲ Many conductors use a small thin stick called a baton to keep time and bring in musicians.

PLAYING THE ORCHESTRA

The conductor also brings musicians in, giving them a signal to start playing at the right time. During the piece, the conductor moves their hands, body, and face to show the orchestra how to perform the music—big movements for loud music, and smaller, gentle ones for soft music. The conductor is also responsible for leading the orchestra in rehearsal, helping them both to learn the piece and put the necessary expression into their performance.

BEAT PATTERNS

Conductors keep time by moving their hand or baton in set beat patterns. To conduct two beats in a bar, they would make a shape like a banana: down, up, down, up. For three beats in a bar, they beat in a triangular shape, with each corner signifying a beat: down, right, up. For four beats, the shape is a bit like an upside-down letter T: down, left, right, up. The first beat is always down, and the last beat is always up. This is why the last beat of a bar is called the "up beat" and the first one the "down beat."

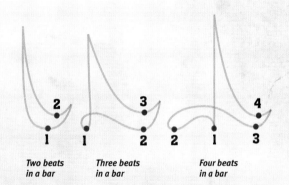

Two beats in a bar

Three beats in a bar

Four beats in a bar

The choir

A choir is a group of people all singing together. The number of people in a choir can range from fewer than 10 to more than 100. A small choir is sometimes called a "chamber choir." The different sections of the choir sing at different pitches creating chords, or harmony.

HIGH AND LOW

A standard choir is made up of four sections, who each sing notes within a certain range of pitches. These are:

Soprano: High female voices
Alto: Low female voices
Tenor: High male voices
Bass: Low male voices
Musicians often refer to music written using these parts as "SATB," meaning "soprano, alto, tenor, and bass."

SINGING ALONE

Often a choir will be accompanied by a piano, organ, or orchestra. Sometimes, however, a choir can sing without any musical accompaniment. This is known as *"a cappella"* singing and dates back centuries (see Medieval music on page 26). The term *"a cappella"* means "in a church style," because this style of singing was first developed for Christian worship.

BOY SOPRANO

A boy whose voice has not yet broken can sing soprano too, although he is usually known as a treble (or sometimes a "boy soprano"). Treble voices are often featured in church choirs. Once his voice breaks in his early teens, he will then usually sing either tenor or bass instead. A man who is able to sing the alto parts is known as a countertenor.

◀ *A young boy singing in a choir.*

▲ *The Romanian choir, Nasterea Domnului, performs at the World Choir Games in 2014.*

21

Expression markings

While the symbols on the stave tell the musician the pitch and length of the notes, most written music also contains terms, called expression markings, that show *how* the music should be played. These relate to the **dynamics** and tempo of the piece.

▶ *Musicians can use a metronome to keep a steady tempo.*

▲ *A statue of Guido de Arezzo, the Italian monk who invented the stave in the 11th century.*

ITALIAN STYLE

Expression markings are usually written in Italian (or as abbreviations of Italian words). This is because Italy was one of the main birthplaces of classical music, where many of the early musical rules were established.

DYNAMICS

Crescendo (get gradually louder)

Diminuendo (get gradually softer)

Pianissimo (very soft)

Piano (softly)

Mezzo piano (quite soft)

Mezzo forte (quite loud)

Forte (loud)

Fortissimo (very loud)

pp	Quieter
p	
mp	
mf	
f	
ff	Louder

TEMPO

Slower ——————————————————————— Faster

| **Lento** (very slow) | **Adagio** (slow) | **Andante** (walking pace) | **Allegretto** (quite fast) | **Allegro** (fast) | **Presto** (very fast) |

The science of music

When an instrument is played, the vibrations travel as sound waves through the air to reach our ears (see page 7). In a large concert hall or church, the sound waves bounce off the walls, creating an echo or reverberation. Many concert halls have devices called acoustic diffusers which absorb some of the sound waves and reduce these reverberations.

▲ Mushroom-shaped diffusers were attached to the ceiling of the Royal Albert Hall in London to reduce its echo.

MAKE IT LOUDER

All musical instruments need a **resonator** to make their sound louder and fuller. A piano has a large wooden soundboard, a xylophone has resonating tubes beneath its keys, and a drum has a rounded, hollow body which amplifies the vibration of the drum skin. In stringed instruments, such as the violin (left), the sound resonates through a hollow wooden body.

ELECTRONIC HELP

Electric instruments, such as the electric guitar (above), don't need resonators. Their sound is amplified electronically, and is relayed through speakers instead.

Music through the ages

Orchestral music has undergone huge changes over the past 1,500 years. For much of this period, the music became more complex while orchestras grew larger, culminating in the vast productions of the Romantic era. However, in the 20th century, there was a reaction against these trends.

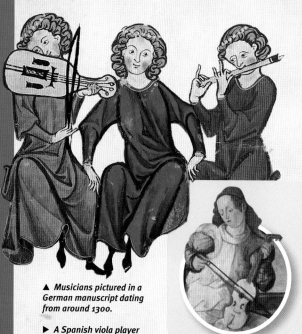

▲ Musicians pictured in a German manuscript dating from around 1300.

▶ A Spanish viola player in around 1500.

MEDIEVAL ERA

This period saw many of the innovations that would lead to the development of the modern classical orchestra. Music began to be written down for the first time and new instruments were invented.

RENAISSANCE ERA

Music grew more complex during this period as people in Europe took a great interest in the arts inspired by ancient Greece and Rome. Harmonies began to be used and musical pieces grew longer.

BAROQUE ERA

In this era, many art forms grew in complexity. Buildings (particularly churches) were elaborately decorated while music became ever more sophisticated and ambitious.

◀ A wooden Baroque recorder.

500–1400 Medieval	1400–1600 Renaissance	1600–1740 Baroque
Music is characterized by simple songs and instruments but is beginning to grow more complex (see page 26).	Polyphonic singing is invented and several new instruments are introduced (see page 27).	Key signatures, time signatures, and dynamic marks are invented and the harpsichord becomes a major instrument (see pages 28–29).

The gemshorn was a Medieval instrument a bit like a recorder but made from animal horn.

▲ The form of the modern orchestra took shape during the Classical era.

CLASSICAL ERA

This period saw the rise of great composers, such as Mozart, as orchestral music became based on memorable melodies. Once played mainly in church and by the aristocracy, music began to reach more ordinary people at this time.

20TH CENTURY

In the 1900s, composers started to challenge all the established rules of music, rejecting conventional chords, melodies, instruments, and structures to try to create sounds that were wholly new—and sometimes very strange.

ROMANTIC ERA

Romanticism was highly expressive with big orchestras creating big sounds for very long pieces of music. Much of the orchestral music of this time—as well as the numerous ballets and operas—was written to create an emotional response in the listeners.

▼ Actors and singers perform the opera Parsifal *by the Romantic composer, Richard Wagner.*

1740–1800 Classical
The piano becomes the primary keyboard instrument and the symphony becomes a popular musical form (see page 30).

1800–1900 Romantic
Big, brash music that tells a story dominates the age as the genres of opera and ballet come to the fore (see page 31).

1900–2000 20th Century
Music becomes more experimental, while the traditional orchestra gets a new lease of life in film music (see pages 32–35).

14

Medieval music 500–1400

In Medieval times, European music sounded very different from how it does today. Monks in churches and abbeys worshipped by singing plainsong—a single line of music sung quite slowly and with a free rhythm. The most popular type of plainsong was called Gregorian chant. The monks would sing these chants *a cappella* (without musical accompaniment).

▼ *Modern re-enactors perform as a medieval group, which would have traveled between towns entertaining the local people.*

ORAL TRADITION

Most songs in early Medieval times were learned by oral tradition—hearing someone else sing and then copying them. But it was also during this time that music first started to be written down. To begin with, *neumes* (pronounced "nyooms") were used. These were lines and dots above the words to show the general shape of the melody—where it goes up and down. Over time, the practice of writing notes on a set of horizontal lines (the stave) to give the exact pitch was developed.

▲ *A 14th-century piece of music using four stave lines rather than five.*

Renaissance music 1400–1600

The Renaissance was a time of great creativity in the fields of literature, architecture, art, and music. Vocal music became more complex, as songs were written with several different interweaving parts, all meant to be sung at the same time. This is known as polyphonic singing.

▶ Shawms came in different sizes to play different ranges of notes. This musician from around 1500 is playing the largest shawm, the bass.

INSTRUMENTS

It was during the Renaissance that the four voices of soprano, alto, tenor, and bass were first classified. A greater variety of musical instruments was also used to accompany the singing, as well as to perform purely instrumental pieces. These included:

• The shawm—a woodwind instrument with a double reed, similar to the oboe.

• The sackbut—the ancestor of the modern trombone.

• The lute—a stringed instrument similar to a guitar, but with around 15 strings, mostly tuned in groups of two.

• The Renaissance flute—similar to today's flute but made out of wood instead of metal.

◀ Musicians play lutes in this painting entitled The Concert from 1623.

Renaissance means "rebirth" and refers to a revival of interest in ancient cultures.

Baroque music 1600–1740

Music in the Baroque period grew increasingly sophisticated and ornate. Composers created complicated melodies and began using key signatures and time signatures more regularly. Dynamics like *piano* and *forte* also started to be used.

THE HARPSICHORD

Baroque times saw the growing popularity of the harpsichord, a keyboard instrument that is the ancestor of the piano. When a key is pressed on a harpsichord, it makes a small quill pluck a string inside the instrument. In the Baroque period, harpsichords could have two keyboards, one above the other. The black and white keys were also often colored the opposite way around to the way they are today.

▲ *Harpsichords were often ornately decorated.*

CHAMBER MUSIC

During this period, chamber music became popular. This was music played by a small ensemble of perhaps four or five musicians. It was often performed at private venues, such as larger houses or palaces (the word "chamber" means "room").

EARLY TRUMPET

The orchestras in Baroque times were usually quite small, often with only one instrument playing each part. The trumpets at this time did not have valves, and so could only play certain notes (see page 10).

▼ A modern chamber ensemble consisting of two violins, a viola, and a cello (known as a string quartet).

COMPOSERS

The most celebrated Baroque composer was Johann Sebastian Bach (1685–1750) from Germany, who composed hundreds of pieces for keyboard, choir, and orchestra. Other famous composers of this period include the Italian Antonio Vivaldi (1678–1741), who wrote more than 500 concertos (see page 30), and the German-British George Frederic Handel (1685–1759), who composed many works for orchestra and choir.

▼ The Baroque composers Johann Sebastian Bach (left) and George Frederic Handel.

Classical music 1740–1800

The term "classical music" is often used to describe all orchestral music, but it can also be used to refer specifically to music written between 1740 and 1800—the Classical period. Classical music was more tune-based than Baroque and often played by large orchestras.

▼ The most famous composer of the age was the Austrian, Wolfgang Amadeus Mozart (1756–1791), pictured here performing as a child (center).

MUSICAL DEVELOPMENT

Certain forms of music became popular in Classical times. These included the symphony, an orchestral piece in four sections (called movements), and the concerto. The concerto features an orchestra and a soloist (a single player) and is made up of three movements: a fast movement, then a slow one, and finishing with another fast one.

NEW INSTRUMENTS

This period also saw the development of new instruments, such as the clarinet and the piano. The piano uses wooden hammers covered with felt to hit the strings when a key is pressed. This means a piano can be played loudly or softly, depending on how hard the keys are hit. The instrument's original name was "*forte-piano*" which means "loud-soft" in Italian.

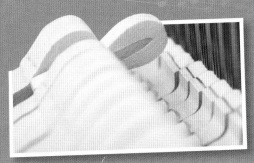

▲ The felt-covered hammers of a piano.

Romantic period 1800–1900

In the Romantic period, the orchestras became much larger, sometimes containing as many as a hundred musicians playing together. The music composed during this time was often loud and dramatic, expressing lots of strong emotions.

BALLET

Composed to accompany a story told through dance, ballet music grew more popular in this era. The Russian Tchaikovsky (1840–1893) wrote three famous ballets: *Swan Lake*, *The Sleeping Beauty*, and *The Nutcracker*.

TELLING A STORY

Music of the Romantic era often told a story. For example, the French composer Saint Saëns (1835–1921) wrote *Danse Macabre* ("Gruesome Dance"), which describes skeletons rising from their graves and dancing at midnight. Czech composer Bedrich Smetana (1824–1884) wrote *Vltava*, a piece describing the journey of a river.

OPERA

Opera, a type of intense drama in which all the parts are sung, also became popular at this time. Famous Romantic operas include *The Barber of Seville* by the Italian Rossini (1792–1868) and *Carmen* by Bizet.

▼ *A scene from* Carmen, *a Romantic opera by the French composer Bizet (1838–1875).*

STRAUSS

Johann Strauss II of Austria composed hundreds of waltzes, including *Wiener Blut* ("Viennese Blood") and *The Blue Danube*, which is named after an Austrian river.

▲ *Johan Strauss (1825–1899) was known as the "Waltz King."*

Twentieth century 1900–2000

In the 20th century, many composers tried to do new and different things, pushing the boundaries of what music is and how it is made. They did this by experimenting with unusual rhythms, chords, melodies, and time signature changes.

▼ A 2016 performance of The Rite of Spring by Igor Stravinsky (1882–1971).

OUTRAGE AND UPROAR

In 1913, a performance in Paris of Igor Stravinsky's *The Rite of Spring*, an orchestral work for ballet, caused outrage. The audience was shocked to hear a work that experimented with tone, meter, and **dissonance**, and the uproar drowned the music. Today, *The Rite of Spring* is seen as one of the most influential works of the 20th century.

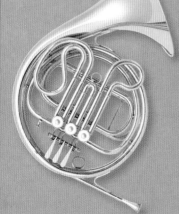

TEACHING MUSIC

Not all new compositions were designed to shock the audience. The Russian Sergei Prokofiev (1891–1953) wrote *Peter and the Wolf* to try to teach children about music. The score tells a story with each character played by a different instrument: Peter is played by the violins, the wolf is represented by the French horns, while the bassoon takes the part of Peter's grumpy grandfather.

◄ The wolf's theme is played on three French horns.

Written in 1952, John Cage's 4'33" consists of four minutes and 33 seconds of silence.

▼ A fight scene from the original production of West Side Story in 1957.

JAZZ

Jazz (see pages 40–41) started to influence composers during this period. These included George Gershwin (1898–1937) from the USA, who wrote *Rhapsody in Blue* in 1924, a jazzy composition for piano and orchestra. His fellow American Leonard Bernstein (1918–1990) wrote *West Side Story* in 1957, a jazz-influenced retelling of William Shakespeare's play *Romeo and Juliet*.

▲ A 1945 poster for a film about the life of George Gershwin.

FAR OUT

In 1917, English composer Gustav Holst (1874–1934) completed *The Planets*, a musical piece describing most of the planets in our Solar System.

ATONAL MUSIC

Some 20th-century music is "atonal," which means it does not have a standard key signature and may use unusual chords. The purpose is to create new, strange-sounding melodies that are very different to **tonal** music.

MINIMALISM

Minimalism, which began in the USA, is a style of music that uses simple musical phrases, called motifs, that are repeated over and over, often on mallet instruments, such as the marimba or xylophone. As they repeat, the motifs slowly alter or shift their timing to create interesting effects. Some of the most famous minimalist composers are the Americans Steve Reich, John Cage (1912–1992), and Phillip Glass.

▶ Phillip Glass, pictured in 2007, at the age of 80.

Film music

Music in films provides much more than just a theme tune or an accompaniment to the credits. It also helps to tell a story and creates the right mood for what is happening on screen, for example building tension, anticipation, excitement, sadness, fear, or relief.

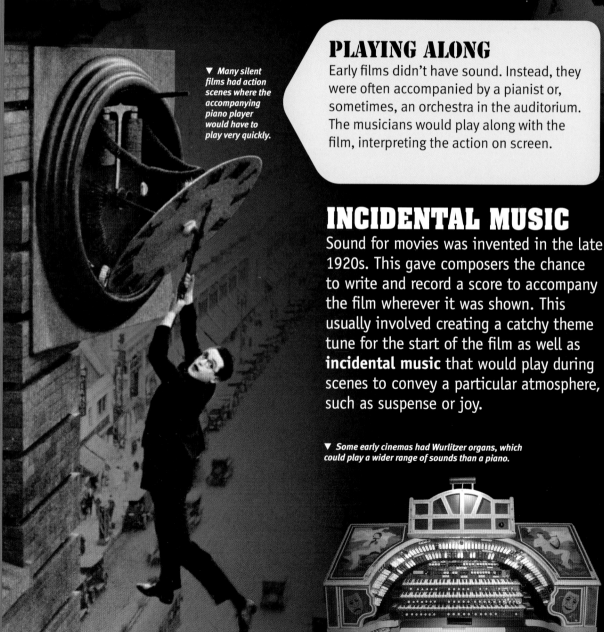

▼ Many silent films had action scenes where the accompanying piano player would have to play very quickly.

PLAYING ALONG

Early films didn't have sound. Instead, they were often accompanied by a pianist or, sometimes, an orchestra in the auditorium. The musicians would play along with the film, interpreting the action on screen.

INCIDENTAL MUSIC

Sound for movies was invented in the late 1920s. This gave composers the chance to write and record a score to accompany the film wherever it was shown. This usually involved creating a catchy theme tune for the start of the film as well as **incidental music** that would play during scenes to convey a particular atmosphere, such as suspense or joy.

▼ Some early cinemas had Wurlitzer organs, which could play a wider range of sounds than a piano.

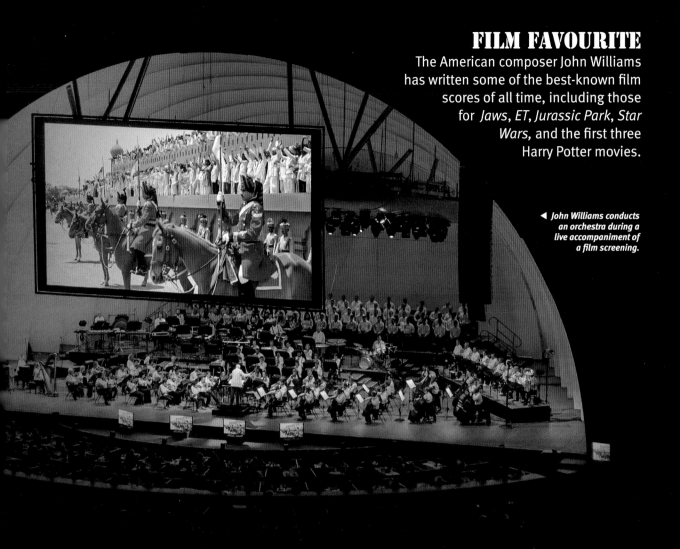

FILM FAVOURITE

The American composer John Williams has written some of the best-known film scores of all time, including those for *Jaws*, *ET*, *Jurassic Park*, *Star Wars*, and the first three Harry Potter movies.

◄ *John Williams conducts an orchestra during a live accompaniment of a film screening.*

TIMING

Nearly all modern films have a musical score. The music is written to fit each scene and must be carefully recorded so it exactly matches the action. In contrast, some animated films, such as Disney's *Fantasia* (1940), were carefully put together so the action exactly matched existing pieces of music.

▲ *Erich Wolfgang Korngold (1897–1957) won two Oscars for his film scores in the 1930s.*

COMPOSER

One of the most successful current film composers is Hans Zimmer. Born in Germany in 1957, he now lives in the USA, where he has written many film scores, including *Pirates of the Caribbean*, *Interstellar*, and *Kung Fu Panda*.

► *Composer Hans Zimmer at the Los Angeles premiere of the movie* Interstellar, *in 2014.*

Musical genres

Music comes in a whole range of styles, known as "genres." Some genres are highly distinctive, while others share similarities with others. In each case, the rhythm, melody, chords, and instruments combine to create the genre's particular sound.

▲ *The guitarist Manuel Granados playing flamenco, a traditional Spanish genre of music.*

ORIGINS

Many factors contribute to the sound of a particular genre, including the country and culture of its origin. Sometimes a style of music is so heavily influenced by the place of its birth that it becomes permanently associated with it—such as jazz with New Orleans, salsa with Cuba, or flamenco with Spain.

▲ *A jazz band performs while marching down a street in the home of jazz, New Orleans, in 1962.*

▼ *Rhythm in Bronze, a Malaysian fusion band who combine traditional gamelan music with more modern sounds, performing in 2009.*

African Influences
Blues, gospel, and jazz all have their roots in African-American culture (see pages 38–41).

R&B and soul
These fusion styles brought together different influences to forge new sounds (see page 42).

Country
Country music grew out of the traditional folk music of Irish and Scottish settlers in the USA (see page 43).

Rock and heavy metal
The guitar is the main instrument in rock and heavy metal music (see pages 44–46).

TIME

The period when a genre of music is created also has a major influence on how it sounds. A style that was invented 10 years ago will sound very different from one that began 100 years ago.

◀ *The genre of ragtime popularized by Scott Joplin (1867–1917) was cutting-edge in 1900, but now sounds quite old-fashioned.*

FUSION

Often a new musical genre is created by blending two or more existing styles—this is called a **fusion**. For instance, rock and roll began in the early 1950s as a mixture of rhythm and blues and country music. Some fusions happen naturally over time, while others are the result of a deliberate mixing of styles, such as jazz-funk, folk-rock, or jazz-gospel.

▲ *The trumpeter Miles Davis (1926–1991) explored many genres during his long career.*

Reggae
The music from Jamaica became known around the world in the 1960s and 1970s (see page 47).

Pop music
Pop music constantly changes with the times to reflect what is currently popular (see pages 48–49).

Rap and hip hop
The spoken rhymes of rap emerged in New York City in the 1970s (see page 50).

House
DJs use various pieces of technology to create the electronic dance music of house (see pages 51).

Blues

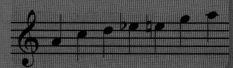

Blues emerged in the southern United States at the start of the 20th century. It's a fusion of African rhythms and melodies, brought over by slaves during the 17th and 18th centuries, and European-American folk music.

BIRTH OF THE BLUES

The songs brought to America by African slaves used the five-note **pentatonic** scale, which formed the basis of the blues scale. These African melodies gradually blended with European chords and the blues was born.

SCALE

Blues melodies are based on a sequence of notes called the blues scale, which is slightly different from a standard major or minor scale.

12 BAR

Blues is always in **4/4 time** and uses a particular sequence of repeating chords, called the 12-bar blues progression.

▲ *A blues scale in A.*

MELANCHOLY MUSIC

Blues songs are often about sadness, loneliness, poverty, or other misfortunes. This reflected the harsh lives of the early blues artists, many of whom were former slaves. Their emotions came through in their songs.

◄ *The American folk and blues singer Huddie William Leadbetter (1888–1949), better known as Lead Belly, played many instruments, including the guitar and accordion.*

◄ *Bessie Smith (1894–1937) was a popular blues singer of the 1920s.*

CHANGING TIMES

Early blues was often performed by just a singer with an acoustic guitar. Later on, blues bands that used electric instruments emerged.

◄ *B.B. King (1925–2015), one of the pioneers of electric blues, performing in 1971.*

"I Got the Blues" by Antonio Maggio was the first blues song to be published, in 1908.

Gospel

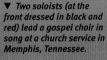

FIVE NOTES

Many well-known gospel songs still use the pentatonic scale, including "Swing Low, Sweet Chariot" and "Amazing Grace."

Gospel music also has its roots in black American culture. It began in churches where African slaves sang songs called spirituals. Over time, these spirituals were blended with traditional European and American hymn tunes to create a vibrant singing style using four-part harmony.

CALL AND RESPONSE

Gospel choirs often use a musical device called "call and response." This is where the solo singer performs a line, and then the whole choir responds. It's quite common for gospel choir singers to learn their songs by heart, rather than reading from sheet music.

▼ *Two soloists (at the front dressed in black and red) lead a gospel choir in song at a church service in Memphis, Tennessee.*

Jazz

As with blues, jazz is a mixture of African-American and European-American musical influences, which emerged in the city of New Orleans, Louisiana, in the early 20th century. Unlike classical music, jazz features a lot of improvisation. But jazz musicians don't just make up random melodies—they improvise their parts using the chords and notes of a set musical framework.

▲ The American big band leader and clarinettist Benny Goodman (1909–1986) in 1946.

SWING

In the 1930s, a new type of jazz called swing emerged that was played by groups called "big bands." These were much larger than the early jazz groups, featuring several trumpets, trombones, and saxophones (known as the "horns"). These were accompanied by a rhythm section and usually a vocalist. Artists like Duke Ellington, Glenn Miller, and Benny Goodman had famous big bands, who played songs such as "In the Mood," "Take the A Train," and "Tuxedo Junction." As with all jazz, the frontline musicians would improvise their solos.

DIXIELAND

Early jazz in New Orleans was also known as Dixieland jazz. The bands at this time usually featured a trumpet, a clarinet, and a trombone as the main solo instruments (known as the "front line"). These could be accompanied by a banjo or guitar, drums, and a double bass or tuba (known as the "rhythm section"). There was often a vocalist too, and the bands played simple tunes like "O When the Saints Go Marching In" or blues songs.

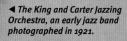

◄ The King and Carter Jazzing Orchestra, an early jazz band photographed in 1921.

▲ *Dizzy Gillespie (left, 1917–1993), one of the main bebop musicians, performs with his band in 1946.*

BEBOP

In the 1940s, a third style of jazz known as bebop became popular. Bebop music was designed to be listened to, rather than danced to, and rarely contained vocals. The groups were small, and the musicians' improvisations were faster and more complex than what had gone before and often used unusual chords and melodies.

ARMSTRONG

Born in New Orleans, Louis Armstrong (1901–1971) was one of the key figures of 20th-century jazz. With his inventive trumpet playing and distinctive gravelly singing voice, he performed from the 1920s to the 1960s.

▶ *Louis Armstrong's career included concerts, recordings, and movies.*

NEW STYLES

From the 1950s onward, jazz split into several sub-genres. These included the quiet, laid-back tones of West Coast jazz and the loud, clashing sounds of free jazz in which musicians improvised "freely," ignoring formal musical rules. The trumpeter Miles Davis, widely regarded as one of the most influential jazz musicians of last century, explored numerous genres in the 1960s and '70s including the fusion music, jazz-funk.

◀ *Two of jazz's most celebrated performers, Charlie Parker (left, 1920–1955) and Miles Davis, play in 1947.*

25

R&B and soul

R&B, which stands for "rhythm and blues," began in the USA in the 1950s. This early style of R&B was quite different from the more modern form of the genre. It was a fast-paced, energetic form of music heavily influenced by gospel, jazz, and blues.

▲ *The singer James Brown (1933–2006) was known as the "Godfather of Soul."*

ORIGINAL R&B

The R&B music of the 1950s and '60s had a strong beat, usually in 4/4 time, which made it good to dance to. It was typically played by a small band made up of a singer, backing singers, a piano, a guitar, bass, drums, and saxophone.

NEW R&B

A new form of R&B developed in the 1980s, which mixed the original sounds with soul, funk, and pop. Some of the most successful R&B artists of this time included Stevie Wonder, Michael Jackson, and Whitney Houston.

SOUL

Soul music also emerged in the 1950s. It is another fusion style, blending elements of R&B, gospel, and blues. The music often focuses on the passionate, "soulful" performances of the singers. In the 1960s and '70s, new dance-oriented forms of soul called funk and disco also emerged.

◀ *Sam Cooke (1931–1964) and Aretha Franklin were two of the leading soul artists of the 1960s.*

Country music

Originating in the Appalachian Mountains of the USA in the 1920s, country music has its roots in Irish and Scottish folk music. The songs almost always feature vocals, which usually tell a story. The music is also often characterized by duets in harmony and has a relaxed feel.

INSTRUMENTS

Guitar, double bass, and harmonica are commonly used in country music, as is the banjo, particularly in an offshoot of the genre called bluegrass. The song melodies in country are often quite simple and tend to be based around just three or four different chords, but can often be made to sound richer via the use of sung harmonies.

▲ *A guitar player can use the steel to perform a glissando up or down the strings.*

STEEL GUITAR

Originating on the island of Hawaii, the steel guitar is a slightly unusual instrument often featured in country music. It's designed to be played horizontally (either sat on the musician's lap or held in a frame). The musician uses one hand to slide a thin metal bar called a "steel" up and down the strings to change the notes while plucking or strumming with the other hand.

▶ *Dolly Parton pictured in 1983.*

COUNTRY ARTISTS

Country artists, such as Glen Campbell, John Denver, Kenny Rogers, and Dolly Parton, became very popular in the 1960s and '70s. Recent stars, who perform a more pop-influenced form of this music, include Shania Twain and Taylor Swift.

◀ *Taylor Swift pictured in 2007.*

Rock music

The guitar-oriented genre of rock began life in the 1950s as rock and roll. This was a fusion of several styles, including R&B, country music, and the blues. A typical rock and roll band consisted of a singer, one or two guitars, bass guitar, and drums.

▲ Elvis Presley (1935–1977) has sold more records than any other rock and roll singer.

EVOLUTION

Early rock and rollers, such as Chuck Berry, Little Richard, and Jerry Lee Lewis, played short, fast-paced songs with simple arrangements. Almost all songs used a 4/4 time signature. In the 1960s, rock and roll began to evolve. Bands such as the Beatles in the UK and the Beach Boys in the USA began employing different instruments—sometimes including whole orchestras—and advanced recording techniques to create more complex songs.

SEVENTIES

By the 1970s, rock and roll was known simply a "rock" and was characterized by its strong beat and loud sound. Many new genres started to emerge. Progressive rock bands, for example, wrote long, complicated songs designed to show off their musicianship.

▶ Formed in 1960, British rock group the Beatles became one of the most influential bands of all time. They split up in 1970.

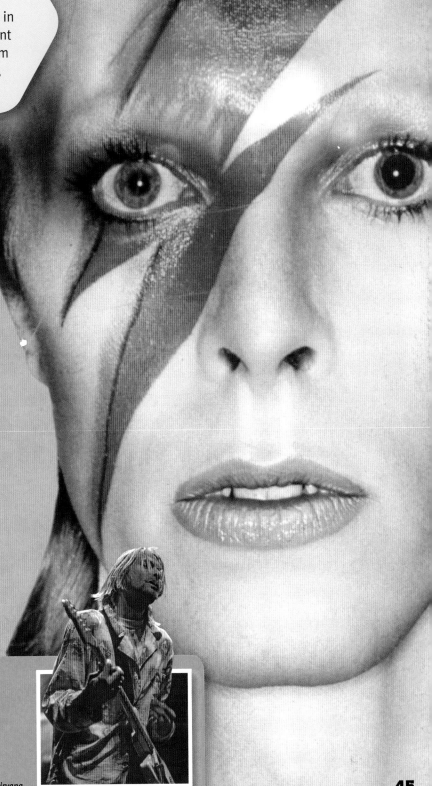

GLAM

The 1970s also saw the emergence of glam rock in the UK. This was a short-lived but very popular genre in which artists dressed in flamboyant costumes and wore make-up. Glam rock artists included David Bowie, Queen, and Roxy Music.

▶ *The singer and musician David Bowie (1947–2016) during the glam rock era.*

PUNK

Punk is a rebellious form of rock featuring short, loud songs often with shouted lyrics. It began in the late 1970s partly as a reaction against the long, complicated music of progressive rock.

▲ *The Clash, a British punk band, in 1977.*

GRUNGE

New rock genres have continued to appear, including grunge in the 1990s which turned the band Nirvana into stars.

▶ *Kurt Cobain (1967–1994), lead singer of Nirvana.*

Heavy metal

Heavy metal is a form of rock music that developed in the UK and USA in the late 1960s and '70s. As the name suggests, the music has a "heavy" sound built on driving guitar lines, pounding drums, and wailing vocals.

GUITAR SOLOS

The guitar is the main instrument of heavy metal with many songs based on riffs—repeating guitar lines. Guitar solos are also common, giving guitarists the chance to show their skills by playing fast, complicated passages. During these solos, they often play the high-pitched notes at the top end of the guitar neck.

MORE STYLES

Since the 1970s, heavy metal has evolved into many different styles. Some bands, such as Led Zeppelin in the 1970s, play softer ballads, as well as hard, rocking songs. Others play particularly fast and loud forms of the genre with names such as speed metal or thrash metal.

▼ *Led Zeppelin performing in 1977.*

▼ *A guitarist can use the dials on a pedal to set their desired level of distortion.*

DISTORTION

Usually, musicians don't want to have distortion, which happens when the music is amplified too loud for the speakers, affecting its sound quality. A distorted sound is more blurred and buzzy than a pure sound. But in heavy metal, guitar distortion is a vital part of the sound. Musicians use special distortion pedals to achieve the effects they want.

Reggae

Reggae originated on the Caribbean island of Jamaica in the 1970s. It developed out of earlier styles including rock steady and ska.

OFF BEAT

Reggae features elements of R&B, blues, and jazz as well as African rhythms and Caribbean styles, such as calypso. It is characterized by strong chords played by the guitar on the off beat, while the bass guitar plays on the beat, creating what are known as "broken chords."

◀ A piece of reggae music showing the chords played on the off beats.

MARLEY

The most famous and influential reggae artist was Bob Marley. With his band, the Wailers, he achieved worldwide fame in the 1970s with his catchy and often politically themed songs. His best-known compositions include "No Woman No Cry" and "One Love."

▶ Bob Marley (1945–1981) performing in 1978.

DUB

Over time, reggae has branched out into a number of different styles. These include the bass and drum-heavy form, dub, and the dance-oriented style, dancehall.

AFRICAN REGGAE

Reggae is also popular in Africa, with artists such as Alpha Blondy of the Ivory Coast and Tiken Jah Fakoly in Mali. They blend reggae with traditional African music.

▶ Tiken Jah Fakoly in 2011.

The Bob Marley album *Legend* is the best-selling reggae album of all time.

30 ▶ Pop music

Pop music can refer both to any music with mainstream appeal and also to "pop," a specific genre that emerged out of rock and roll in the 1950s. Pop songs are usually quite short and are designed to be catchy and enjoyable.

SUPERSTARS

From Elvis Presley in the 1950s to Michael Jackson (1958–2009) and Prince in the 1980s and Beyoncé in the 2010s, the biggest pop stars have often been among the most famous people on Earth.

▲ *Madonna is the biggest selling female pop star of all time.*

STYLES

Pop is performed both by bands and solo artists. The music doesn't have a set style and songs don't always feature the same instruments. Rather, the style and instrumentation change with the times to reflect contemporary trends. The music tends to focus on the singing and the songs are often about love and relationships. The beat is almost always in 4/4 time.

▼ *The pop star Justin Bieber performing in New York City in 2015.*

MANUFACTURED POP

Pop music is often designed to appeal to a young audience. This is especially true of "manufactured" pop bands whose members don't come together through their own choice, but are picked by record companies—or sometimes on talent shows—because they have a sound (and look) with huge appeal to young people. Manufactured bands include the Monkees in the 1960s and One Direction in the 2010s.

▲ The Spice Girls, a popular manufactured pop band, were formed in 1994 and released their first single in 1996.

▶ Prince (1958–2016), one of the biggest pop stars of the 1980s, on stage in 1985.

STRUCTURE

Most pop songs follow a similar pattern. They tend to start with a brief musical intro (short for introduction) before the singer comes in. There will then usually be a couple of alternating verses and choruses. The chorus is the most important section, as this contains the "hook," or catchy part, which the listener goes away singing in their head (and which persuades them to buy the song). Some pop songs also include a bridge, a short part that is different from both the verse and chorus, as well as an "outro"—like an intro, but at the very end of the piece.

49

Rap and hip hop

Rap is a form of music in which the words are not sung, but are rather chanted or spoken over the music. It began in New York City in the 1970s and formed part of a wider culture of street dance, fashion, and graffiti art that became known as hip hop.

▶ The US rapper Snoop Dogg on stage in 2009.

SAMPLING

Rappers don't normally perform with a band. Instead they make their rhymes over short, repeated sections of existing songs called samples played by someone with a turntable known as a DJ. Sometimes rappers improvise their rhymes— this is known as freestyling.

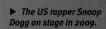

TAKING THE WORLD BY STORM

In the 1980s, rap grew into a global phenomenon with artists such as Run DMC, Public Enemy, and MC Hammer becoming famous. More recent artists have included Eminem, Kanye West, and Kendrick Lamar.

With more than 150 million albums sold, Eminem is the best-selling rap artist.

50

House

House is a type of electronic music that started in Chicago in the 1980s. The music is created using lots of technology including synthesized bass lines, sampled sounds, and programmed drum rhythms. The drums include a characteristic "four to the floor" beat, where the bass drum is played on every beat of the bar.

LIVE EXPERIENCE

When performing live, a house DJ will use decks (a pair of record turntables), a crossfader, and other equipment to mix tracks together.

32

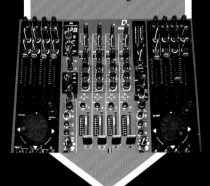

◄ A sound mixer, which can be used to blend samples together.

DESIGNED FOR DANCE

Sampling and the repetition of short melodies are also common features of this music, which is designed to be played in clubs for people to dance to. Famous house artists include Moby, Calvin Harris, Avicii, and the Swedish House Mafia. There are many similar types of electronic music related to house, including techno and garage.

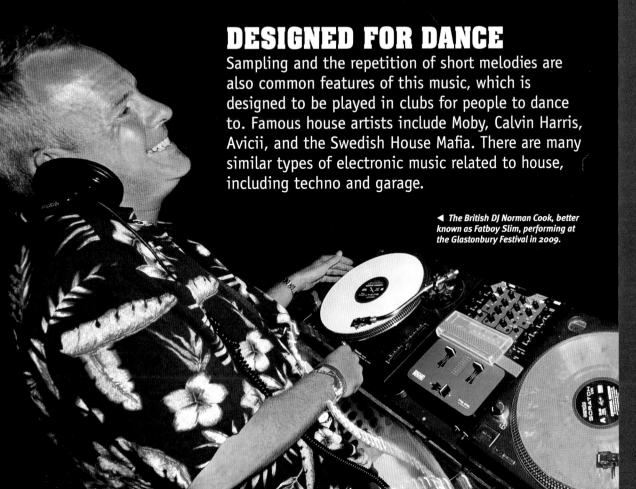

◄ The British DJ Norman Cook, better known as Fatboy Slim, performing at the Glastonbury Festival in 2009.

Released in 1984, "On and On" by Jesse Saunders is considered the first house record.

51

Music from around the world

Although music is often said to be a "universal language," every culture has different ways of making and understanding music. In the West, music that isn't from the USA or Europe is often referred to by the single term, "world music." But world music encompasses a vast array of different styles, sounds, and approaches to making music.

▼ Frances Densmore, an ethnomusicologist with the Smithsonian Museum in Washington, D.C., listening to a recording with a Native American leader, Mountain Chief, in 1916.

ETHNOMUSICOLOGY

The word "ethnomusicology" means "the study of the music of different cultures." Someone who studies music from around the world is called an ethnomusicologist. An ethnomusicologist will usually travel to different (and sometimes very remote) places to find out about how the people there make music and why. They will also find out what instruments are used, how they are played, what music means to the local people, and how it is learned.

Folk
The traditional music of the people has enjoyed a revival in recent years (see pages 54–55).

Native North American
This music has been passed down the generations over thousands of years (see page 56).

Aboriginal
Australian Aboriginal musicians utilize circular breathing to play the didgeridoo (see page 57).

African
Africa has produced a wide variety of musical styles, many based on drumming (see page 58–59).

INSTRUMENT CATEGORIES

Instruments used to make music in other countries are often quite different from those found in a Western orchestra or rock band. There may be similarities, but they can't always be categorized using standard terms such as brass, woodwind, or strings. Instead, ethnomusicologists break instruments down into four main types based on how their sound is made:

▶ *Russian balalaika*

AEROPHONES

These are instruments that use air to make a sound. This is usually breathed from the mouth, like bagpipes, but a pipe organ is also an aerophone.

▲ *Scottish bagpipes*

CHORDOPHONES

These are instruments that have strings that vibrate to make the sound. This includes many varieties of lute, harp, and violin.

IDIOPHONES

These are instruments that do not have skins or strings, but which vibrate when hit, scraped, or shaken, such as castanets, maracas, or cowbells.

◀ *Spanish castanets*

MEMBRANOPHONES

These are instruments that have a skin that vibrates when struck to make a sound. This includes almost all drums.

▶ *African djembe*

 **Latin & Caribbean**
Numerous dance-oriented styles have emerged from these regions (see pages 60–63).

Chinese & Japanese
The music of both China and Japan is often based on the pentatonic scale (see pages 64–65).

Indian
Indian melodies are based on scales called ragas (see page 66).

Indonesian
Gamelan orchestras perform using sets of tuned percussion instruments (see page 67).

Folk music

In the 1960s, folk music was fused with rock to form a new style: folk-rock.

Across the globe, the traditional music of each nation is known as its "folk" music. The word "folk" means "people," so folk music is the music of the people. It often dates back hundreds of years and features traditional songs which have been passed down generations by oral tradition.

▶ A Celtic folk band with an array of traditional instruments and drums.

CELTIC ROOTS

▲ A group of bagpipe players in Scotland.

Today, some of the most popular folk music is the Celtic music of Scotland and Ireland. Celtic music is also played in Brittany in France, Galicia in Spain, and Portugal. The instruments in Celtic folk include the fiddle (violin), bagpipes, penny whistle, a type of drum called the bodhrán (pronounced "bough-rawn"), and the harp.

POLITICAL MESSAGE

Folk melodies sometimes take the form of lively dances known as jigs. They are also often written in modes—special scales that existed before our modern major and minor scales were invented, and use different gaps (or intervals) between each note. Many folk songs tell stories about the history and beliefs of the local folk community and some have a political message.

HURDY-GURDY

Often featured in European folk music, the hurdy-gurdy is a curious instrument which has been around since the Renaissance. The player turns a handle at one end which turns a wheel. The wheel then rubs against two outer strings to play a **drone**, while vibrating three other strings that run up through the centre of the instrument. When the player then presses one of the instrument's keys, a small wooden post known as a tangent presses against one of the three strings to create a certain pitch.

◀ *An ornate 19th-century hurdy-gurdy.*

FOLK REVIVAL

Despite its old-fashioned sound, folk music has enjoyed a revival in recent times with groups such as The Corrs, Bellowhead, Mumford & Sons, and Lucy Spraggan all producing successful folk or folk-influenced music.

▼ *The English folk singer Laura Marling performing in 2012.*

Native North American music

The traditional folk music of the First Nations people of Canada and the Native Americans of the USA dates back thousands of years, long before Europeans colonized these lands. The music is still very much alive today, having been passed on by oral tradition down through the generations.

▼ A Native American musician playing a six-holed flute.

SCALES

Native American music uses both the five-note pentatonic scale and the tetratonic scale, which has just four different pitches (see below).

Although the styles can vary greatly across North America, the music is often linked to religious ceremonies or important cultural events and involves both solo and group singing.

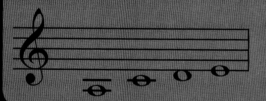

▲ A round-framed drum being beaten at a pow-wow.

POW-WOW

A common characteristic of Native American music is a strong and regular drum beat played on a round-framed drum. These days, traditional North American music is celebrated at a pow-wow, a large cultural gathering involving music, costume, and dance.

Aboriginal music

In Australia, the music of the indigenous people, also known as Aboriginal Australians, features a number of instruments. These include pieces of wood known as clapsticks that are beaten against each other to produce a rhythm.

DIDGERIDOOS

The most famous Aboriginal instrument is the didgeridoo (pronounced "did-jerry-do"). It is played like a brass instrument by vibrating the lips against one end. This creates a single-pitched drone, although the player can change the tone of the sound by altering the shape of their mouth. Didgeridoos are made from the branches of eucalyptus trees.

▶ An Aboriginal Australian performs with a didgeridoo. The biggest didgeridoos can be up to 10 feet long.

CIRCULAR BREATHING

Skilled didgeridoo musicians employ a very unusual technique to play their instrument known as circular breathing. This involves the player breathing out air stored in their cheeks while breathing in new air through their nose at the same time. When mastered properly, circular breathing allows the player to produce a continuous sound on the instrument.

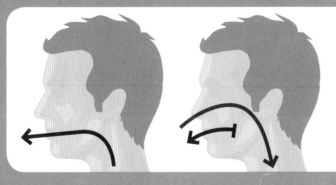

1. Breathe out through your mouth and fill up your cheeks.

2. Blow out from your cheeks and breathe in through your nose.

3. Repeat.

African music

Each of the 54 African countries has its own particular ways of making and experiencing music. However, there are features that are common across much of the continent. The music is often characterized by **syncopated** drumming that blends different rhythmic patterns together to create an exciting layered effect. Many songs are based on the pentatonic scale and employ call and response singing.

MUSIC OF THE NORTH

The musical traditions of the countries in North Africa differ from those of the African countries south of the Sahara. In the north, Arabic music dominates, which is a primarily vocal style using lots of heavily decorated musical phrases and featuring traditional instruments such as the rahab (a sort of small violin) and the oud (a type of lute).

Famous African musicians include Youssou N'Dour of Senegal and Salif Keita from Mali.

▶ *Traditional dancers move to the music at a wedding in Kenya.*

DRUMMING

There are many different types of drum in Africa. One of the most common is the djembe (pronounced "jem-bay"), which is played with both hands and can produce different sounds depending on which part of the skin is hit. Another drum, the double-headed talking drum, is held under the arm and squeezed, which changes the pitch of the sound by tightening the drum skins. It's also called the talking drum because it sounds a little like a human voice going up and down. The drums of Burundi in East Africa sometimes have a head measuring more than 3 feet across. They are played by groups of 12 or more, all positioned in a circle with the leader in the center. As they play, the musicians chant loudly and often dance, leap, and perform other gymnastic feats.

▲ Burundi drummers use sticks to hit the drum, both on its skin and on the sides.

OTHER INSTRUMENTS

In addition to traditional drums, African musicians perform using many other types of instrument. Here are just a few:

BALAFON

Common in West Africa, the balafon is the ancestor of the xylophone or marimba. It is made of differently pitched wooden bars that are hit with beaters.

KORA

The kora is a 21-stringed harp. The strings are arranged in two rows and are played with the thumbs and first fingers only. It originated in West Africa.

MBIRA

The mbira, or thumb piano, consists of a number of thin metal strips fixed to a resonator, each one tuned to a different pitch. The musician uses both thumbs, alternating between them to play a melody.

NGONI

The ngoni has four strings and is the ancestor of the modern banjo.

EVENT SONGS

In sub-Saharan Africa, many of the traditional songs are linked to certain events, such as weddings, harvests, hunting, or building a house.

◄ The famous South African trumpeter, Hugh Masekela.

The largest steel pan concert took place in 2012, featuring 400 drummers and 1,000 pans.

Steel drums (or pans) were first made on the small islands of Trinidad and Tobago in the Caribbean. In the late 1800s, the then British rulers banned the use of traditional wooden drums. However, the local people (whose music originated in Africa) were determined to keep playing their rhythms, so they began to use other materials to make their instruments, including old discarded oil drums.

▲ *The flag of Trinidad and Tobago.*

MAKING A PAN

To make the drum, the round top of an oil drum (originally its base) is carefully beaten into a series of dents using a hammer. Each dent is a slightly different size, giving it a different pitch. The name of each pitch is then painted onto the drum so that the player can identify them. A steel drum ensemble can include several different drums that together form chords and harmony. The band is usually accompanied by other untuned percussion, including drums and shakers.

▶ *Steel drums are played with wooden sticks tipped with rubber.*

BOSSA NOVA

Bossa nova is a popular Latin style where the focus is more on the tune than the percussion, although the melodies can still be very syncopated. The Brazilian Astrud Gilberto has been a famous bossa nova singer since the 1960s, known for her renditions of "The Girl from Ipanema" and "Fly Me to the Moon."

◄ *The Brazilian bossa nova singer Astrud Gilberto performing in 1966.*

Latin music

Latin music combines Spanish guitars, African rhythms, and European chords to create an energetic and syncopated sound. It is played throughout Central and South America, but the forms that have come out of Cuba, Brazil, and Argentina are particularly well-known.

CLAVE

Many forms of Latin music, including salsa, rumba, and mambo, are based on short syncopated rhythmic patterns called *claves* (pronounced "clah-vays").

▶ *Salsa musicians play on a Cuban back street in 2013.*

SALSA

Although the term "salsa" originated in New York in the 1970s, the dance-based music is based on Latin rhythms, particularly son, cha cha cha, and mambo from Cuba. According to one story, it acquired its name because it is a mixture of several different styles, just as salsa is a sauce made from many ingredients. It is one of the most well-known kinds of Latin music. A typical salsa band will include trumpets, saxophones, and conga drums.

TANGO

Tango began in Argentina in the late 19th century. It is both a form of syncopated music and a dance performed by two people dancing close together. A traditional tango ensemble includes a violin, a double bass, a guitar, and an accordion.

Samba drumming

Samba is an energetic form of Latin music from Brazil based on African rhythms. A samba band is mainly made up of drummers who play fast-paced syncopated rhythms on a variety of percussion instruments. Samba provides the main musical accompaniment to the world's biggest carnival in Rio de Janeiro, Brazil.

▲ A group of samba drummers performing at the UK's Notting Hill Carnival.

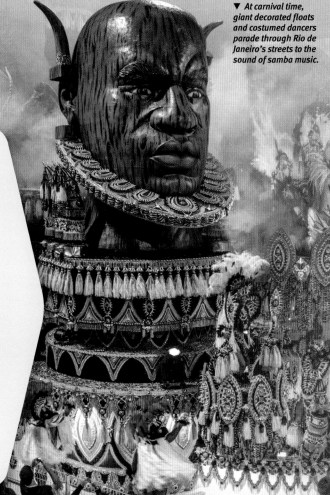

▼ At carnival time, giant decorated floats and costumed dancers parade through Rio de Janeiro's streets to the sound of samba music.

PATTERNS

Samba pieces usually begin with a call and response section, when the band leader will play a short drum pattern and the rest of the band will respond. The music will then settle into a repeated groove with all the musicians playing. At a certain point, the leader will blow a whistle and give hand signals to show the band a break is coming. This is a short section, different from the main groove, which adds variety. In a break, the entire band often plays the same rhythm, whereas in the groove there are many different rhythmic patterns, known as polyrhythms.

THE SURDO

The heartbeat of the samba rhythm is provided by the surdo—a large double-headed barrel drum made of light metal. Surdos come in three sizes, small, medium, and large, which have high, medium, and low pitches. The drums are played with large soft beaters.

REPENIQUE

The repenique (pronounced "heh-pen-ee-kay") looks like a very small surdo, but it has a much tighter skin which enables it to play a bright, high-pitched sound. The band leader will usually play the repenique to begin the samba, as it is the loudest instrument in the band. Samba bands also feature a Brazilian snare drum called a caixa (pronounced "ka-i-sha").

OTHER PERCUSSION

Agogo bells are very important in a samba ensemble. They are made up of two metal bells—one larger than the other—which play repeating patterns, moving between the two different pitches. The agogo is hit with a wooden stick.

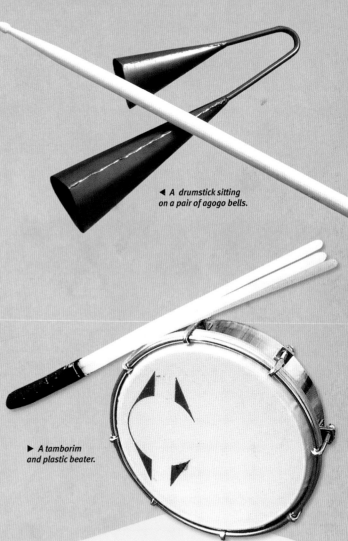

◄ *A drumstick sitting on a pair of agogo bells.*

▼ *The two thin metal strips stretched across the caixa give it its "snare" sound.*

▲ *A medium-sized surdo drum with a beater resting on top.*

▶ *A tamborim and plastic beater.*

GANZA

Small tube-shaped shakers called ganzas add to samba's rhythmic feel.

TAMBORIM

Small drums called tamborims are hit with thin plastic sticks. The tamborim looks a bit like a small tambourine but it doesn't have any bells around the edge.

Chinese music

Traditional Chinese music dates back thousands of years and is very different from the folk music of Europe or the USA. It doesn't use chords and harmony and can be quite slow. However, it does share one similarity with Western folk styles in that it tends to use the pentatonic scale.

Chinese music doesn't usually follow a steady beat like Western music.

INSTRUMENT CATEGORIES

Chinese music is made with many different instruments. Some look quite similar to Western ones, while others are very unusual:

ERHU

The erhu (pronounced "ur-hoo") is the Chinese equivalent of the violin. It has only two strings and the bow is set between them. The hexagonal resonator is quite small and covered in snake skin which vibrates to make the sound. The neck is narrow and does not have any frets.

PIPA

The pipa is a four-stringed instrument a bit like a lute. It has lots of frets and is played both on its own as a solo instrument and in groups.

SHENG

The sheng, also known as the free reed harmonica, works a bit like a miniature pipe organ (see pages 76–77). The player blows into a small air chamber and then places fingers on holes near the bottom of 17 bamboo pipes. When a finger covers one of these holes, it causes air to blow across the reed for that pipe, making it vibrate and sound a note.

YANGQIN

The yangqin (pronounced "yang-chin") consists of a number of strings stretched tightly over a wooden frame which are hit with two rubber-tipped bamboo beaters.

▲ An erhu

◀ A pipa

▼ A musician blowing into the base of a sheng.

Japanese music

As in China, traditional Japanese music is often based on the pentatonic scale. It may feature large, double-headed drums called taiko, which are played with two sticks. The drums are normally placed on a stand with the skins facing sideways, making them easier to play.

◀ A musician playing a large taiko drum mounted on a stand.

▲ A musician in traditional dress playing a shamisen.

SHAMISEN

The shamisen is a three-stringed instrument played a bit like a guitar or lute. However, it has no frets on the neck, so the player has to learn the positions for each note. Although a famous Japanese instrument, the shamisen originally came from China, where it is called the sanxian and is still played today.

◀ A 19th-century painting of a Japanese shakuhachi player.

SHAKUHACHI

The shakuhachi (pronounced "sha-koo-hatch-ee") is a Japanese bamboo flute that usually has five holes: four at the front, and one at the back for the thumb. It doesn't have a reed or mouthpiece like a clarinet or a recorder. Instead, the player blows across a diagonal hole at one end. The shakuhachi can produce a large range of pitches and tone qualities.

Kodo are a famous Japanese taiko group who have performed around the world.

43

Indian music

Traditional Indian music incorporates a range of styles, tempos, and scales. Typically, drums will be used to create repeating rhythmic patterns called talas. An ornate melody—often improvised—is played over the top using an Indian scale known as a raga. Different ragas are used to create a variety of moods.

DRUM PAIRS

Tabla drums are always played in pairs: the daya is smaller and played with the right hand, while the baya is larger and more rounded and played with the left hand. There are various techniques for playing, including tapping the skins with the fingertips or slapping them with the whole hand. Tabla rhythms can be very complex and fast.

SITAR

One of the main Indian melodic instruments, the sitar is a bit like a guitar or lute, but has around 20 strings. Only six or seven of these strings are used for playing the melody. The other strings are made up of two drone strings to add extra texture and up to 13 "sympathetic" strings, which vibrate when the melody strings are played, but are never played directly themselves.

◀ *The sitar has lots of movable frets along its neck to help the musician play different scales.*

HARMONIUM

The harmonium is a small keyboard instrument which was originally brought over to India from Europe in the 19th century. It has since become an important part of the country's musical culture. Bellows at the back of the instrument push air through metal reeds which make the sound.

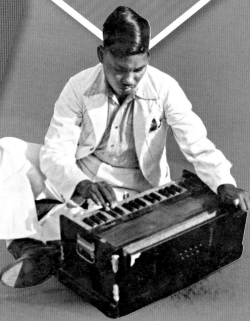

▲ *A musician playing a harmonium in 1949, just after India gained independence from Britain.*

Gamelan

The word "gamelan" is Indonesian for "to hit with a hammer." It has also become the name of the set of percussion instruments used by orchestras on the Indonesian islands of Java and Bali. These instruments are struck with hammers or beaters.

◄ Two-headed Kendhang drums provide the main rhythm in a gamelan orchestra.

▲ An Indonesian musician playing gamelan gongs set on wooden stands.

CULTURAL ROLE

Gamelan is often played as part of religious or cultural ceremonies. For instance, it might be used to accompany a dancer or a shadow puppet play. The music uses the pentatonic scale and is based upon a repeated core-melody, which is usually eight beats long. The whole ensemble is led by the kendhang drummer, although it will always follow the movement of the dancer or shadow puppeteer.

GONGS

The melodies in gamelan music are played both on kettle-shaped gongs and metallophones, which are made up of long metal bars set over resonator tubes and look a bit like large glockenspiels. Extra percussion is provided by several suspended gongs and two or three barrel-shaped drums known as kendhang.

► A traditional Balinese dancer performs to gamelan music.

Amazing instruments

Although the instruments that make up the modern orchestra are largely fixed, new instruments are still being invented. Some are adaptations, improvements, or even just enormous versions of existing instruments. Others are completely new concepts.

▲ One of Harry Partch's more unusual creations, the Gourd Tree and Cone Gongs, is a percussion instrument.

▲ A musician playing a daxophone at a German jazz festival in 2015.

THE DAXOPHONE

The German experimental musician Hans Reichel (1949–2011) invented a new idiophone in the 1980s. Called the daxophone (to rhyme with saxophone), it consists of a curved piece of wood attached to a resonator and is played with a double bass bow. It produces a strange, haunting sound.

HARRY PARTCH

The American Harry Partch (1901–1974) was a composer and musical theorist who invented numerous unusual instruments. These included a 10-string guitar, a marimba made of light bulbs, and a unique 44-stringed instrument known as a harmonic canon.

◀ Like all Harry Partch's instruments, his bamboo marimba was set to a special tuning of his own devising.

Amazing instruments
Musicians and inventors have come up with some unusual instruments over the years (see above).

Groovy guitars
Some guitars have more than one neck, giving them a versatile sound (see pages 70–71).

Peculiar pianos
Keyboard instruments have gotten steadily smaller over the centuries (see pages 72–73).

WEATHER MUSIC

Some inventors have harnessed the weather to help them play instruments. This has seen the creation of an enormous wind-played sculpture, the Singing Ringing Tree, in Lancashire, England, and a giant sea organ in Zadar, Croatia. This consists of a number of tubes built into the town's sea wall which play notes when waves force water into them.

◄ Wind entering the pipes of the Singing Ringing Tree can produce eerie sounds.

▲ A hydraulophone is played a little bit like a piano.

WATER MUSIC

Water has been used in musical instruments for centuries—the ancient Romans had an organ powered by flowing water. However, the US inventor Steve Mann has taken the concept a few steps further with his hydraulophone, or water organ, where players touch jets of water to change notes.

GIANT INSTRUMENTS

There is lots of competition for the title of the world's largest instrument. However, the winner is probably the Earth Harp, a giant instrument with strings that can be stretched hundreds of feet to attach to the outside of an auditorium—this means that the audience actually stands inside the instrument as it plays.

Bizarre brass
Not all brass instruments are made of brass (see page 74).

Funky flutes
The flute may be the original melodic instrument (see page 75).

The pipe organ
The pipe organ is the world's loudest acoustic instrument (see page 76–77).

Groovy guitars

Everyone is familiar with what a guitar looks like. Both the acoustic type, with its hollow wooden body, and the solid-bodied electric version are featured in music across the globe. But there are also some much more unusual—and less frequently used—guitars.

MANY STRINGS

A double-necked guitar is a versatile instrument. Each of its necks has a different set of strings; perhaps twelve strings on one and six on the other, or four bass strings on one and six treble strings on the other. The player can switch between either neck, depending on the kind of sound required.

▲ A double-necked guitar dating back to 1690.

▲ A 12-string guitar needs 12 separate tuning pegs.

12 STRINGS

A 12-stringed guitar is like a jazzed-up version of a traditional six-stringed one. Its 12 strings are set out in six pairs, with each pair tuned to the same note as on a six-stringed guitar. However, each of the lowest four pairs of strings is tuned an octave apart, to give the instrument a richer, fuller sound, which makes it very well suited for strumming chords.

▲ Pat Metheny playing the Pikasso guitar in 2012.

▲ George Harrison played a 12-stringed electric guitar on many of The Beatles' songs.

MANY NECKS

The very unusual-looking Pikasso guitar goes a couple of steps further than the double-necked version with various different playing options. It contains four different sets of strings, two sound holes, and a total of 42 strings. It was invented for the guitarist Pat Metheny in 1984 and took two years to build. It consists of one normal guitar neck with six strings, two shorter necks with 12 strings each (although not in pairs, as you would expect), and some harplike strings on the opposite side of the instrument, which can also be strummed. It is named after the Spanish artist, Pablo Picasso, who was famed for his paintings of strange-looking figures with limbs and features in unusual places.

RESONATING

Resonator guitars date back to the 1920s, and were built to try to create a louder sound in the era before electric guitars had been invented. Instead of being made of wood, the guitar body is made either partly or completely of metal. In place of a sound hole is a large cone-shaped resonator, which increases the volume and also gives the guitars a distinctive sound.

▶ A six-stringed resonator guitar.

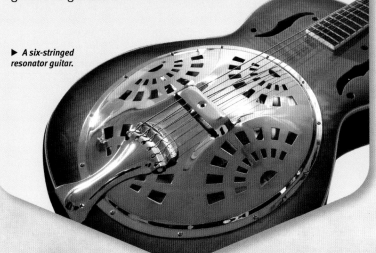

Peculiar pianos

There are two main types of piano: grand pianos and upright pianos. Grand pianos are larger and louder, making them suitable for playing with orchestras, and have strings arranged horizontally in overlapping parallel rows. The strings in the smaller, quieter upright piano run vertically almost from the floor up to the top of the instrument. To save space, the strings also cross over each other. But these differences don't tell the whole story. There's also plenty of variety in the piano world.

SMALLER AND SMALLER

Over the centuries, keyboard instruments have shrunk dramatically in size. A traditionally made concert grand piano can be over 10 feet long and weigh over 1,100 pounds. However, technological advances have led to the creation of small, lightweight keyboards that can be carried with one hand.

▲ A late 19th-century player piano—the roll of paper has been punched with holes that tell the instrument which notes to play.

PLAYER PIANOS

The player piano or pianola, which was invented in the late 1800s, removed the need for a pianist altogether. Instead the music was played automatically. A mechanical device inside the instrument could read a roll of thick paper punched with holes to tell it which keys needed to be played and when. It was popular for a few decades, but improvements to recording technology in the 1920s ended

BOGÁNYI PIANO

One of the most recent innovations in piano technology
is the futuristic-looking Bogányi piano. It was invented
by a Hungarian pianist called Gergely Bogányi, and is
made out of carbon fiber instead of wood to make it
less susceptible to moisture. Its curved edges have
been designed to help project the sound directly at the
audience and it boasts a special "floating" soundboard
which allows notes to be held for longer.

GIRAFFE PIANOS

Before the upright piano was invented in the early 19th
century, only grand pianos were available, and they took up a
lot of room. One early attempt to save floor space was the
giraffe piano, which was basically a vertical grand piano.

▶ An early 19th-century giraffe piano.

Bizarre brass

Brass instruments come in all shapes, sizes, and materials— some are not even made of metal. As long as its sound is produced by the player vibrating their lips against the mouthpiece, an instrument is classed as brass.

SERPENT

Dating back to the 1600s, the serpent has a trumpet-like mouthpiece and six finger holes. Although it is made of wood and looks like a woodwind instrument, the playing technique is the same as for a brass instrument. It is called a serpent because its long, curved shape makes it look like a snake.

◀ A 17th-century serpent.

▲ The sousaphone's shape means it can easily be played standing up.

SOUSAPHONE

The sousaphone is popular in the USA, where it is commonly found in marching bands. The tuba plays the same notes but is bulky and difficult to carry. The sousaphone was designed to be worn around the body, making it much easier to handle. It is named after John Philip Sousa, an American composer and band leader, who had the first sousaphones built in 1893 and used them in his own marching band.

ALPHORN

Like the serpent, the alphorn is made of wood but played like a brass instrument. Alphorns can measure over 10 feet long and were once used to send signals between villages in the Alps. Their deep, resonant tones could carry across the wide Swiss valleys where the instrument was invented in the Middle Ages. There are no keys or finger holes on an alphorn—the player can change pitch only by tightening their lips.

▶ Alphorns are so large that they often have to be placed on stands to keep them still while they are played.

Funky flutes

The flute is one of the oldest instruments, dating back to prehistoric times. Across the world, almost every musical culture has developed its own version of the flute.

OCARINA

The ocarina is a vessel flute, which means it has a rounded shape rather than being long and cylindrical. Ocarinas were invented in China thousands of years ago, and are traditionally made from clay. They are played by covering holes on the top of the instrument to change the pitch of the note being blown.

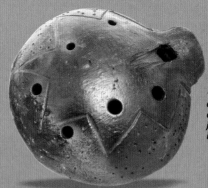

◄ *A small clay ocarina. Most ocarinas are just a couple of inches long.*

PUNGI

The pungi, or been, is a wind instrument found in India and Pakistan and traditionally played by snake charmers. The player blows into a small gourd and the air then vibrates reeds in two different pipes—one plays a drone while the other plays the melody.

▼ *An Indian snake charmer blows into a pungi.*

PAN FLUTES

The pan flute (or pan pipes) is not one flute but a whole set of flutes tied together in a line. The player blows over the top of the pipes (like blowing over the top of a bottle) with each one playing a different note. This means that to play a tune, a player must change from one tube to another, making it difficult to play a fast melody. Pan flutes feature a lot in South American folk music, particularly in Peru.

► *All the individual pipes in a pan flute are different lengths, allowing them to play different pitches.*

The oldest instrument yet found is a 35,000-year-old flute made of bone from Germany.

The pipe organ

The pipe organ is the loudest and largest instrument that can be played by a single person. It consists of hundreds of metal and wooden pipes, which are linked to one or more keyboards (called manuals). Most pipe organs have at least two manuals, which can be played at the same time with each hand. Larger pipe organs can have three, four, or even five manuals, each of which can be set up to make different sounds from the others.

▲ *An organist operating the pipe organ's pedals with their feet.*

PEDALS

Playing the pipe organ is very challenging. As well as manuals, there are also foot pedals laid out like a keyboard. So the organist not only has to use their hands to play different manuals, they also have to play bass notes with their feet at the same time.

▶ *This huge pipe organ towers over the pianos on either side of it.*

PULLING OUT THE STOPS

Inside the casing of the organ, there are several different sets of pipes known as ranks. Each rank of pipes is activated by pulling out a knob next to the keyboard called a stop. Some stops are named after an instrument because the sound made by its rank of pipes resembles that instrument. For instance, some ranks sound like flutes, violins, and even the human voice.

◄ *Labeled stops on a pipe organ: the smaller the number, the higher the pitch.*

LONG AND SHORT PIPES

The numbers on the stops refer to the size of the pipes, measured in feet. The length of each pipe affects how it sounds. A 2-foot pipe makes a high-pitched sound, whereas a 16-foot pipe makes a very low sound. When a stop is pulled out, the air enters the relevant pipe from that rank each time a key on the organ keyboard is pressed. There is one pipe for each key. The air blows across an opening at one end of the pipe in the same way that a flute or a recorder is played.

▶ *Each of these organ pipes will play a slightly different note, depending on its length.*

# GLOSSARY

4/4 TIME
A time signature consisting of four quarter-note beats per bar, giving the music a steady rhythm. It's known as "common time" as it's the most common time signature.

AMPLIFY
To increase the volume of a sound.

BAR
A segment of music corresponding to a repeated pattern of beats. In written music, a bar is marked using vertical lines.

BEAT
The pulse of the music. A piece of music can be divided into individual beats of the same length, which are grouped into bars.

DISSONANCE
A combination of notes that sounds strange and conventionally unharmonious.

DRONE
A note or chord that is sustained continuously throughout a piece of music.

DYNAMICS
How loudly or quietly a note or a group of notes is played.

FRET
A ridge (usually made of metal) on the fingerboard of a stringed instrument marking the position of a note.

FUSION
A blend of two or more types of music.

GENRE
A type of music with a distinct sound that makes it clearly identifiable—and different from other types of music.

GLISSANDO
A rapid slide through a series of notes on an instrument, producing a gliding effect.

HARMONY
Notes of different pitches that are played or sung at the same time to create a conventionally pleasing sound.

INCIDENTAL MUSIC
Music, often without a distinct tune, that plays during a film or TV scene to convey a mood or accompany the action.

KEY
A group of notes used to write a piece of music, which form a scale.

KEY SIGNATURE
Symbols at the start of a piece of written music telling the musician what key the piece is in.

MELODY
A distinctive, often recurring, linear pattern of notes—also known as the tune.

OCTAVE

A pattern of seven ascending (or descending) notes in a scale that repeats every eighth note.

ORCHESTRA

A large group of instrumental musicians. In Western music, they are divided into four main groups: strings, woodwind, brass, and percussion.

PENTATONIC

Describes music made with a scale consisting of five notes instead of the seven that are used in most Western music.

PITCH

How high or low a note is.

QUARTER NOTE

A note length usually corresponding to one beat. It's known as a quarter note because it is one quarter the length of a whole note, which is the longest note usually used in Western musical notation. Quarter notes are also known as crotchets.

RESONATOR

Something that naturally resonates, or amplifies, sound.

RHYTHM

The repeated percussive patterns and notes that give music its feel.

SCALE

A set of notes ordered by pitch. In Western music, the notes usually span an octave.

SCORE

A piece of written music, often featuring the parts for all the individual instruments.

STAVE

A set of five horizontal lines representing different pitches on which notes are written.

SYNCOPATED

Refers to an unexpected change to the normal rhythm of a piece by stressing beats that are not usually stressed.

TEMPO

How quickly or slowly a piece of music is played.

TIME SIGNATURE

Two numbers at the start of a musical piece that show how many beats there are in each bar. The bottom number shows the length of each beat and the top number shows how many beats there are in each bar.

TONAL

Refers to music written in a standard major or minor key, using conventional harmony.

INDEX

Picture credits (t=top, b=bottom, l=left, r=right, c=center, fc=front cover, bc=back cover, i=image)

All images courtesy of *Dreamstime.com* unless otherwise indicated:
Alamy: 5b Roger Cracknell 01/classic, 20–21c Armands Pharyos, 37tr Philippe Gras, 39b Horizons WWP / TRVL, 47cr Pictorial Press Ltd, 49bl Pictorial Press Ltd, 51b Everynight Images, 59cb Pictorial Press Ltd, 66br MEC Collection, 71c Trinity Mirror/Mirrorpix. *Public Domain*: fc line 4 i3, fc line 5 i5, 19tr, 24cl, 26br, 27cl, 27b, 29br, 30cl, 31bl, 33t cl, 34bl, 35cl, 36 cl, 37tl, 38cr br cb, 40b tr, 41t cr b, 44tl, 52–53c. *Shutterstock.com*: bc line 1 i2, 45r. *Wikimedia Commons*: fc line 7 i2 Elijah van der Giessen, 4b Matthias Kabel, 22tr Wilson Delgado, 24b Óscar Romero, 31br Luigi Caputo, 32t KCBalletMedia, 33br WNYC New York Public Radio, 34br Dheckler510, 36br Pepehillo 2010, 42tr jeremy sutton-hibbert, 45cb Pictorial Press Ltd, 46cr Jim Summaria, 46 bl Dhscommtech, 47br Rama, 50cr gcardinal, 55tr Andreas Praefcke, 59tr Dr clave, 59c Jorge Royan, 59cr Charlie Bynum, 59br Lars Curfs, 61tl Kroon, Ron/Anefo, 63cl tr br Alno, 65cl Elijah van der Giessen, 68tr br HorsePunchKid, 68cl Oliver Abels, 69t, 69cl Glogger, 70tr Jorge Royan, 71tr Paul C Hebert, 72bl Daderot, 73t Xinhua, 73br Daderot, 74t Sguastevi.